_To_

_____

From

_____

Occasion

_____

a bouquet of

Timeless Wisdom

 to guide your path

Tyndale House Publishers, Inc.

CAROL STREAM, ILLINOIS

These proverbs will give insight to the simple, knowledge and discernment to the young. Let the wise listen to these proverbs and become even wiser. Let those with understanding receive guidance by exploring the meaning in these proverbs and parables, the words of the wise and their riddles.

PROVERBS 1:4-6

The fear of the LORD is *the beginning* of *wisdom. . . .* The knowledge of the holy is understanding.

PROVERBS 9:10, KJV

Commit yourself
to instruction;
listen carefully
to words of knowledge.

PROVERBS 23:12

My child, listen to me and do as I say, and you will have a long, good life. I will teach you wisdom's ways and lead you in straight paths. When you walk, you won't be held back; when you run, you won't stumble. Take hold of my instructions; don't let them go. Guard them, for they are the key to life.

PROVERBS 4:10-13

My child, pay attention to what I say. Listen carefully to my words. Don't lose sight of them. Let them penetrate deep into your heart, for they bring life to those who find them, and healing to their whole body.

PROVERBS 4:20-22

Wise words are
like deep waters;

wisdom flows
from the wise like a
bubbling brook.

PROVERBS 18:4

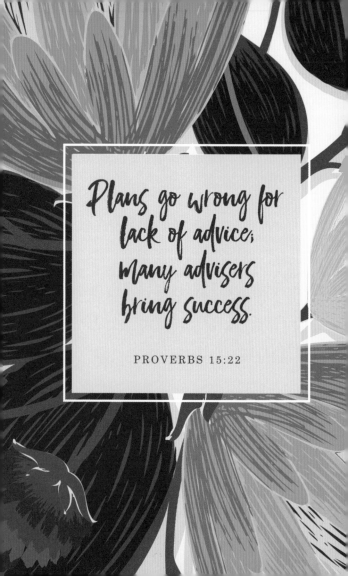

Plans go wrong for lack of advice; many advisers bring success.

PROVERBS 15:22

Two things I ask of you, LORD; do not refuse me before I die: Keep falsehood and lies far from me; give me neither poverty nor riches, but give me only my daily bread. Otherwise, I may have too much and disown you and say, "Who is the LORD?" Or I may become poor and steal, and so dishonor the name of my God.

PROVERBS 30:7-9, NIV

Go to the ant, you sluggard; consider its ways and be wise! It has no commander, no overseer or ruler, yet it stores its provisions in summer and gathers its food at harvest. How long will you lie there, you sluggard? . . . A little sleep, a little slumber, a little folding of the hands to rest—and poverty will come on you like a thief.

PROVERBS 6:6-11, NIV

Better a dry
crust eaten in peace
than a house filled
with feasting—
and conflict.

PROVERBS 17:1

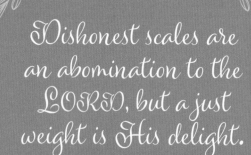

Dishonest scales are an abomination to the LORD, but a just weight is His delight.

PROVERBS 11:1, NKJV

If your enemies are hungry, give them food to eat. If they are thirsty, give them water to drink. You will heap burning coals of shame on their heads, and the Lord will reward you.

PROVERBS 25:21-22

People may be right in their own eyes, but the LORD examines their heart. The LORD is more pleased when we do what is right and just than when we offer him sacrifices.

PROVERBS 21:2-3

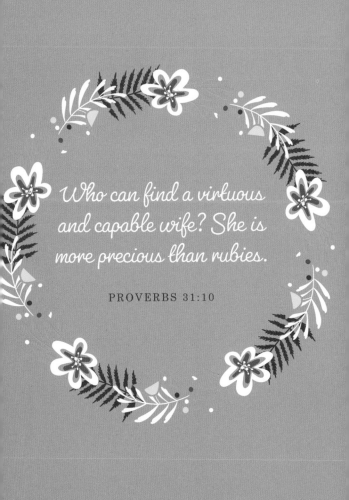

Who can find a virtuous and capable wife? She is more precious than rubies.

PROVERBS 31:10

I, Wisdom,
live together
with good
judgment.
I know

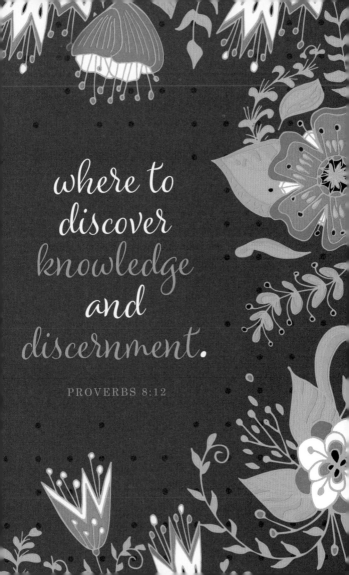

where to
discover
knowledge
and
discernment.

PROVERBS 8:12

Follow my advice, my son; always treasure
my commands. Obey my commands and live!
Guard my instructions as you guard your
own eyes. Tie them on your fingers as a
reminder. Write them deep within your heart.
Love wisdom like a sister; make insight
a beloved member of your family.

PROVERBS 7:1-4

As iron sharpens iron,
so a friend
sharpens a friend.

PROVERBS 27:17

Do not let your
heart envy sinners,
but always be zealous
for the fear of
the LORD.

PROVERBS 23:17, NIV

My son, pay attention to my wisdom; listen

carefully to my wise counsel. Then you

will show discernment. . . . For the lips of

an immoral woman are as sweet as honey,

and her mouth is smoother than oil. But

in the end she is as bitter as poison, as

dangerous as a double-edged sword. Her feet

go down to death; her steps lead straight

to the grave.

PROVERBS 5:1-5

The way of the righteous is like the first gleam of dawn, which shines ever brighter until the full light of day. But the way of the wicked is like total darkness. They have no idea what they are stumbling over.

PROVERBS 4:18-19

Worry weighs a
person down;
an encouraging
word cheers a
person up.

PROVERBS 12:25

The wise conquer
the city of the strong
and level the fortress
in which they trust.

PROVERBS 21:22

Interfering in someone else's argument is as foolish as yanking a dog's ears. Just as damaging as a madman shooting a deadly weapon is someone who lies to a friend and then says, "I was only joking." Fire goes out without wood, and quarrels disappear when gossip stops.

PROVERBS 26:17-20

People who despise advice are asking for trouble; those who respect a command will succeed. The instruction of the wise is like a life-giving fountain; those who accept it avoid the snares of death.

PROVERBS 13:13-14

Choose a good
reputation over
great riches; being
held in high esteem
is better than
silver or gold.

PROVERBS 22:1

The wise store up knowledge, but the mouth of a fool invites ruin.

PROVERBS 10:14, NIV

Speak up for those who cannot speak for themselves; ensure justice for those being crushed. Yes, speak up for the poor and helpless, and see that they get justice.

PROVERBS 31:8-9

To reject the law is to praise the wicked;
to obey the law is to fight them. Evil people
don't understand justice, but those who
follow the LORD understand completely.

PROVERBS 28:4-5

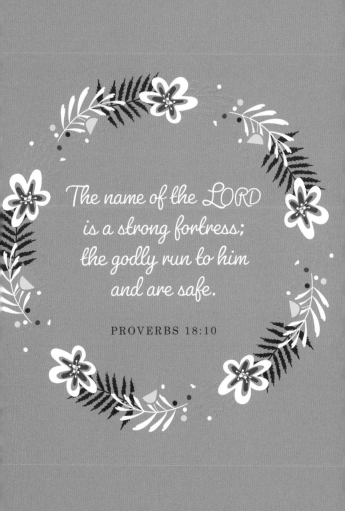

The name of the LORD
is a strong fortress;
the godly run to him
and are safe.

PROVERBS 18:10

The
LORD is
far from the
wicked, but

34

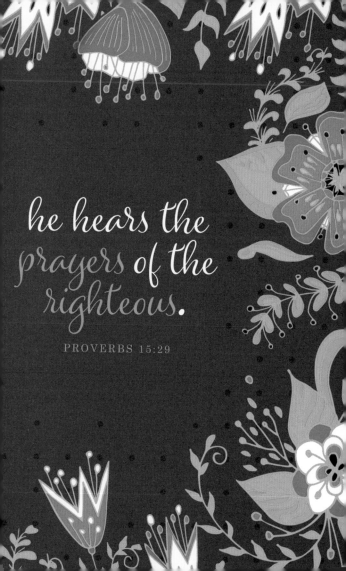

he hears the
prayers of the
righteous.

PROVERBS 15:29

Cry out for insight, and ask for understanding. Search for them as you would for silver; seek them like hidden treasures. Then you will understand what it means to fear the LORD, and you will gain knowledge of God. For the LORD grants wisdom! From his mouth come knowledge and understanding. He grants a treasure of common sense to the honest.

PROVERBS 2:3-7

Better to be
poor and honest
than to be dishonest
and a fool.

PROVERBS 19:1

Spouting off before
listening to the facts
is both shameful
and foolish.

PROVERBS 18:13

Trust in the Lord with all your heart;
do not depend on your own understanding.
Seek his will in all you do, and he will
show you which path to take.

PROVERBS 3:5-6

Remove the impurities from silver, and the sterling will be ready for the silversmith. Remove the wicked from the king's court, and his reign will be made secure by justice.

PROVERBS 25:4-5

Do not boast about
tomorrow, for
*you do not know
what a day
may bring.*

PROVERBS 27:1, NIV

The LORD sees clearly what a man does, examining every path he takes.

PROVERBS 5:21

There are four things on earth that are small but unusually wise: Ants—they aren't strong, but they store up food all summer. Hyraxes—they aren't powerful, but they make their homes among the rocks. Locusts—they have no king, but they march in formation. Lizards—they are easy to catch, but they are found even in kings' palaces.

PROVERBS 30:24-28

Do not be wise in your own eyes; fear the LORD and depart from evil. It will be health to your flesh, and strength to your bones.

PROVERBS 3:7-8, NKJV

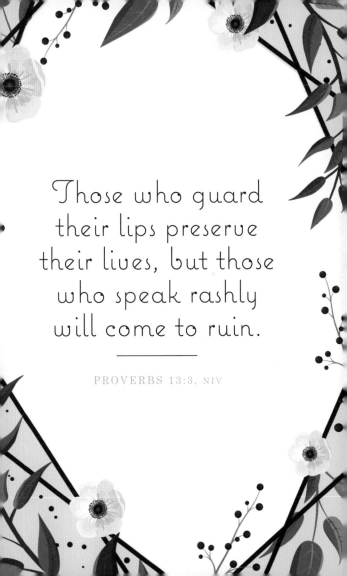

Those who guard
their lips preserve
their lives, but those
who speak rashly
will come to ruin.

———

PROVERBS 13:3, NIV

The wise have wealth
and luxury, but fools
spend whatever they get.

PROVERBS 21:20

Better to have little, with fear for the LORD, than to have great treasure and inner turmoil. A bowl of vegetables with someone you love is better than steak with someone you hate.

PROVERBS 15:16-17

Eat honey, my son, for it is good; honey from the comb is sweet to your taste. Know also that wisdom is like honey for you: If you find it, there is a future hope for you, and your hope will not be cut off.

PROVERBS 24:13-14, NIV

Pride ends in humiliation, while humility brings honor.

PROVERBS 29:23

Justice is a joy to the godly,

but it terrifies
evildoers.

PROVERBS 21:15

Does not wisdom call out? Does not understanding raise her voice? At the highest point along the way, where the paths meet, she takes her stand; beside the gate leading into the city, at the entrance, she cries aloud: "To you, O people, I call out; I raise my voice to all mankind. You who are simple, gain prudence; you who are foolish, set your hearts on it."

PROVERBS 8:1-5, NIV

Wisdom is more
precious than rubies,
and nothing you desire
can compare with her.

PROVERBS 8:11, NIV

The godly walk
with integrity; blessed
are their children
who follow them.

PROVERBS 20:7

The path of the virtuous leads away from evil; whoever follows that path is safe. Pride goes before destruction, and haughtiness before a fall.

PROVERBS 16:17-18

The integrity of the upright will guide
them, but the perversity of the unfaithful
will destroy them. Riches do not profit
in the day of wrath, but righteousness
delivers from death. The righteousness of
the blameless will direct his way aright, but
the wicked will fall by his own wickedness.

PROVERBS 11:3-5, NKJV

Train up a child in the
way he should go. . . .
When he is old,
he will not
depart from it.

PROVERBS 22:6, KJV

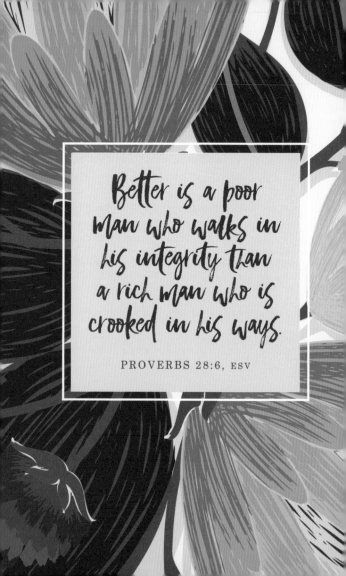

Better is a poor man who walks in his integrity than a rich man who is crooked in his ways.

PROVERBS 28:6, ESV

Never let loyalty and kindness leave you!
Tie them around your neck as a reminder.
Write them deep within your heart. Then you
will find favor with both God and people,
and you will earn a good reputation.

PROVERBS 3:3-4

Those who fear the LORD are secure; he will be a refuge for their children. Fear of the LORD is a life-giving fountain; it offers escape from the snares of death.

PROVERBS 14:26-27

Work brings
profit, but mere talk
leads to poverty!

PROVERBS 14:23

Whoever loves discipline
loves knowledge,
but whoever hates
correction is stupid.

PROVERBS 12:1, NIV

My child, if sinners entice you, turn your back on them! . . . My child, don't go along with them! Stay far away from their paths. They rush to commit evil deeds. They hurry to commit murder. If a bird sees a trap being set, it knows to stay away. But these people set an ambush for themselves.

PROVERBS 1:10, 15-18

Honor the LORD with your wealth and with the best part of everything you produce. Then he will fill your barns with grain, and your vats will overflow with good wine.

PROVERBS 3:9-10

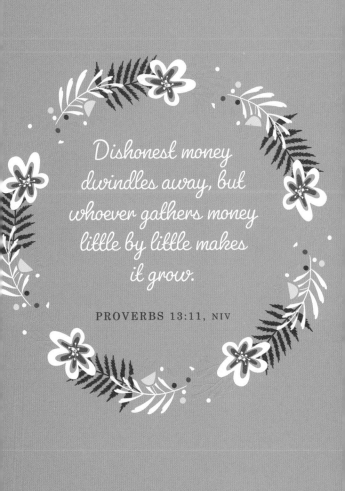

Dishonest money
dwindles away, but
whoever gathers money
little by little makes
it grow.

PROVERBS 13:11, NIV

Trustworthy
messengers
refresh
like snow
in summer.

66

They *revive*
the spirit
of their
employer.

PROVERBS 25:13

Walk in the ways of the good and keep to the paths of the righteous. For the upright will live in the land, and the blameless will remain in it; but the wicked will be cut off from the land, and the unfaithful will be torn from it.

PROVERBS 2:20-22, NIV

Those who trust in
their riches will fall,
but the righteous
will thrive
like a green leaf.

PROVERBS 11:28, NIV

Hatred stirs up quarrels, but love makes up for all offenses.

PROVERBS 10:12

Get wisdom; get insight; do not forget, and
do not turn away from the words of my
mouth. Do not forsake her, and she will keep
you; love her, and she will guard you.

PROVERBS 4:5-6, ESV

A prudent person foresees danger and takes precautions. The simpleton goes blindly on and suffers the consequences. True humility and fear of the L ORD lead to riches, honor, and long life.

PROVERBS 22:3-4

Whoever loves
a pure heart
and gracious speech
*will have the king
as a friend.*

PROVERBS 22:11

Don't say, "I will get even for this wrong." Wait for the LORD to handle the matter.

PROVERBS 20:22

The beginning of wisdom is this: Get wisdom, and whatever you get, get insight. Prize her highly, and she will exalt you; she will honor you if you embrace her.

PROVERBS 4:7-8, ESV

Can a man scoop a flame into his lap and
not have his clothes catch on fire? Can
he walk on hot coals and not blister his
feet? So it is with the man who sleeps with
another man's wife. He who embraces her
will not go unpunished.

PROVERBS 6:27-29

Sensible people
control their temper;
they earn respect by
overlooking wrongs.

———————

PROVERBS 19:11

Every word of God
proves true. He is a
shield to all who come
to him for protection.

PROVERBS 30:5

Don't reject the Lord's discipline, and don't be upset when he corrects you. For the Lord corrects those he loves, just as a father corrects a child in whom he delights.

PROVERBS 3:11-12

My child, if you have put up security for a friend's debt . . . if you have trapped yourself by your agreement and are caught by what you said—follow my advice and save yourself, for you have placed yourself at your friend's mercy. Now swallow your pride; go and beg to have your name erased. Don't put it off; do it now! Don't rest until you do.

PROVERBS 6:1-4

The fruit of the
righteous is a tree of life,
and whoever captures
souls is wise.

PROVERBS 11:30, ESV

Like
a fluttering
sparrow or
a darting
swallow, an

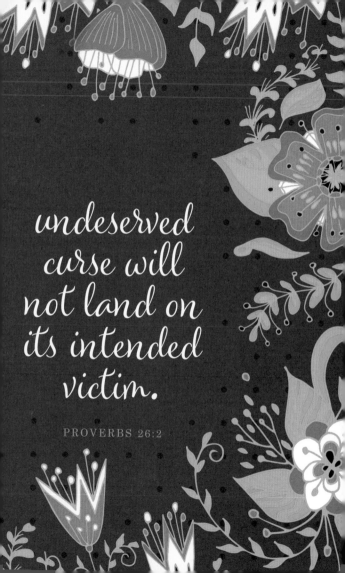

undeserved
curse will
not land on
its intended
victim.

PROVERBS 26:2

Don't lose sight of common sense and discernment. Hang on to them, for they will refresh your soul. They are like jewels on a necklace. They keep you safe on your way, and your feet will not stumble. You can go to bed without fear; you will lie down and sleep soundly.

PROVERBS 3:21-24

The LORD *preserves those with knowledge,* but he ruins the plans of the treacherous.

PROVERBS 22:12

When people's
lives please the LORD,
even their enemies are
at peace with them.

PROVERBS 16:7

Rescue those who are unjustly sentenced
to die; save them as they stagger to their
death. Don't excuse yourself by saying,
"Look, we didn't know." For God understands
all hearts, and he sees you. He who guards
your soul knows you knew. He will repay all
people as their actions deserve.

PROVERBS 24:11-12

Don't bother correcting mockers; they will only hate you. But correct the wise, and they will love you. Instruct the wise, and they will be even wiser. Teach the righteous, and they will learn even more.

PROVERBS 9:8-9

Lazy hands make
for poverty, but
**diligent hands
bring wealth.**

PROVERBS 10:4, NIV

Patience can
persuade a prince,
and soft speech
can break bones.

PROVERBS 25:15

By wisdom the LORD founded the earth; by understanding he created the heavens. By his knowledge the deep fountains of the earth burst forth, and the dew settles beneath the night sky.

PROVERBS 3:19-20

Don't rejoice when your enemies fall; don't be happy when they stumble. For the LORD will be displeased with you and will turn his anger away from them.

PROVERBS 24:17-18

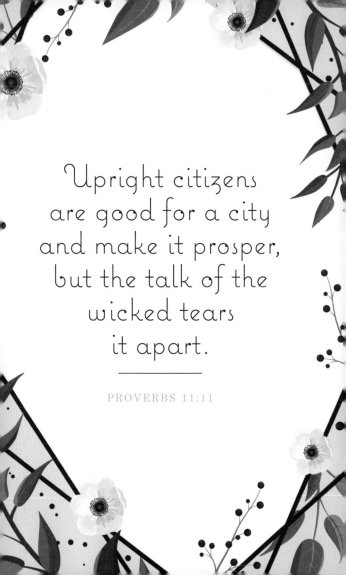

Upright citizens
are good for a city
and make it prosper,
but the talk of the
wicked tears
it apart.

PROVERBS 11:11

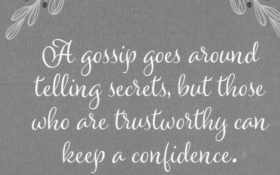

A gossip goes around
telling secrets, but those
who are trustworthy can
keep a confidence.

PROVERBS 11:13

Guard your heart above all else, for

it determines the course of your life.

Avoid all perverse talk; stay away from

corrupt speech.

PROVERBS 4:23-24

The father of godly children has cause for joy. What a pleasure to have children who are wise. So give your father and mother joy! May she who gave you birth be happy.

PROVERBS 23:24-25

The blessing of the LORD
brings wealth, without
painful toil for it.

PROVERBS 10:22, NIV

Tainted
wealth has
no lasting
value, but

*right living
can save
your life.*

PROVERBS 10:2

Timely advice is lovely, like golden apples in a silver basket. To one who listens, valid criticism is like a gold earring or other gold jewelry.

PROVERBS 25:11-12

To discipline a child
produces wisdom,
but a mother is
disgraced by an
undisciplined child.

PROVERBS 29:15

Many are the plans in a person's heart, but it is the LORD's purpose that prevails.

PROVERBS 19:21, NIV

There are six things that the Lᴏʀᴅ hates,
seven that are an abomination to him:
haughty eyes, a lying tongue, and hands that
shed innocent blood, a heart that devises
wicked plans, feet that make haste to run to
evil, a false witness who breathes out lies,
and one who sows discord among brothers.

PROVERBS 6:16-19, ESV

A house is built by wisdom and becomes strong through good sense. Through knowledge its rooms are filled with all sorts of precious riches and valuables.

PROVERBS 24:3-4

If you love sleep,
you will end in poverty.
*Keep your eyes
open, and there will
be plenty to eat!*

PROVERBS 20:13

Don't visit your
neighbor too often,
or you will wear out
your welcome.

PROVERBS 25:17

A gentle answer turns away wrath, but a harsh word stirs up anger. The tongue of the wise adorns knowledge, but the mouth of the fool gushes folly. . . . The soothing tongue is a tree of life, but a perverse tongue crushes the spirit.

PROVERBS 15:1-2, 4, NIV

Don't envy violent people or copy their ways. Such wicked people are detestable to the LORD, but he offers his friendship to the godly.

PROVERBS 3:31-32

Those who love pleasure become poor; those who love wine and luxury will never be rich.

PROVERBS 21:17

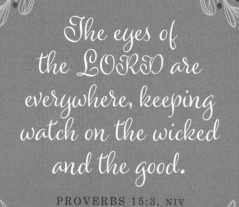

The eyes of
the LORD are
everywhere, keeping
watch on the wicked
and the good.

PROVERBS 15:3, NIV

Don't do as the wicked do, and don't follow the path of evildoers. Don't even think about it; don't go that way. Turn away and keep moving. For evil people can't sleep until they've done their evil deed for the day. They can't rest until they've caused someone to stumble. They eat the food of wickedness and drink the wine of violence!

PROVERBS 4:14-17

A wise man is full of strength, and a man of knowledge enhances his might, for by wise guidance you can wage your war, and in abundance of counselors there is victory.

PROVERBS 24:5-6, ESV

Doing wrong leads to
disgrace, and scandalous
behavior brings contempt.

PROVERBS 18:3

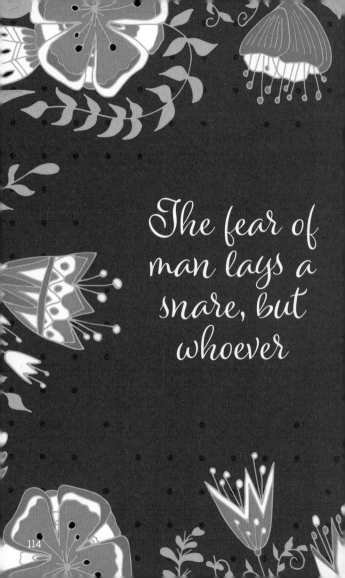

The fear of
man lays a
snare, but
whoever

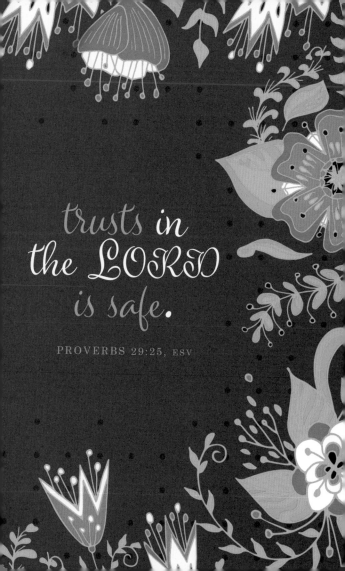

trusts in the LORD is safe.

PROVERBS 29:25, ESV

Blessed are those who find wisdom. . . . Long life is in her right hand; in her left hand are riches and honor. Her ways are pleasant ways, and all her paths are peace. She is a tree of life to those who take hold of her; those who hold her fast will be blessed.

PROVERBS 3:13, 16-18, NIV

A fool is
quick-tempered, but
a wise person
stays calm
when insulted.

PROVERBS 12:16

The crucible for silver and the furnace for gold, but the LORD tests the heart.

PROVERBS 17:3, NIV

Whoever says to the wicked, "You are in the right," will be cursed by peoples, abhorred by nations, but those who rebuke the wicked will have delight, and a good blessing will come upon them.

PROVERBS 24:24-25, ESV

You need not be afraid of sudden disaster or the destruction that comes upon the wicked, for the LORD is your security. He will keep your foot from being caught in a trap.

PROVERBS 3:25-26

Grandchildren are the
crowning glory
of the aged;

parents are the pride
of their children.

PROVERBS 7:16

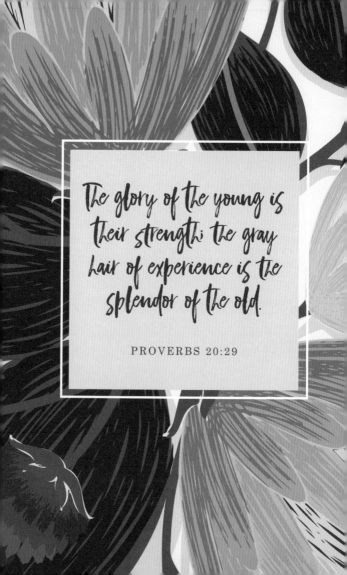

The glory of the young is their strength; the gray hair of experience is the splendor of the old.

PROVERBS 20:29

My son, obey your father's commands, and don't neglect your mother's instruction. Keep their words always in your heart. Tie them around your neck. When you walk, their counsel will lead you. When you sleep, they will protect you. When you wake up, they will advise you.

PROVERBS 6:20-22

Do not withhold good from those who deserve it when it's in your power to help them. If you can help your neighbor now, don't say, "Come back tomorrow, and then I'll help you." Don't plot harm against your neighbor, for those who live nearby trust you.

PROVERBS 3:27-29

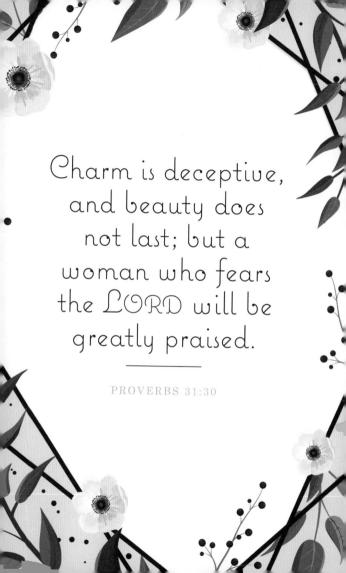

Charm is deceptive, and beauty does not last; but a woman who fears the LORD will be greatly praised.

PROVERBS 31:30

Store my commands in your heart. If you do this, you will live many years, and your life will be satisfying.

PROVERBS 3:1-2

He guards the paths of the just and
protects those who are faithful to him.
Then you will understand what is right, just,
and fair, and you will find the right way
to go. For wisdom will enter your heart, and
knowledge will fill you with joy.

PROVERBS 2:8-10

We can make our plans, but the LORD
determines our steps. . . . We may throw the
dice, but the LORD determines how they fall.

PROVERBS 16:9, 33

Only a fool despises a parent's discipline; whoever learns from correction is wise.

PROVERBS 15:5

A generous
person will
prosper;
whoever

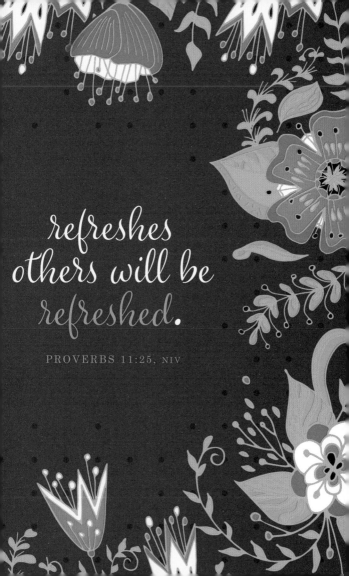

refreshes
others will be
refreshed.

PROVERBS 11:25, NIV

Simpletons turn away from me [wisdom]—to death. Fools are destroyed by their own complacency. But all who listen to me will live in peace, untroubled by fear of harm.

PROVERBS 1:32-33

The house of the wicked
will be destroyed,
but the tent of the godly
will flourish.

PROVERBS 14:11

The LORD directs our steps, so why try to understand everything along the way?

PROVERBS 20:24

Truthful lips endure forever, but a lying tongue is but for a moment. Deceit is in the heart of those who devise evil, but those who plan peace have joy.

PROVERBS 12:19-20, ESV

Discipline your children, and they will give you peace of mind and will make your heart glad. When people do not accept divine guidance, they run wild. But whoever obeys the law is joyful.

PROVERBS 29:17-18

Everyone enjoys
a fitting reply;
it is wonderful to
say the right thing at
the right time!

PROVERBS 15:23

A cheerful heart is good medicine, but a broken spirit saps a person's strength.

PROVERBS 17:22

Don't eat with people who are stingy; don't desire their delicacies. They are always thinking about how much it costs. "Eat and drink," they say, but they don't mean it.

PROVERBS 23:6-7

People who conceal their sins will not
prosper, but if they confess and turn from
them, they will receive mercy.

PROVERBS 28:13

Those who spare
the rod of discipline
hate their children.
Those who love their
children care enough
to discipline them.

PROVERBS 13:24

*A friend loves at
all times, and a brother
is born for a time
of adversity.*

PROVERBS 17:17, NIV

Wise words satisfy like a good meal; the right words bring satisfaction. The tongue can bring death or life; those who love to talk will reap the consequences.

PROVERBS 18:20-21

Whoever walks with the wise becomes wise,
but the companion of fools will suffer harm.
Disaster pursues sinners, but the righteous
are rewarded with good.

PROVERBS 13:20-21, ESV

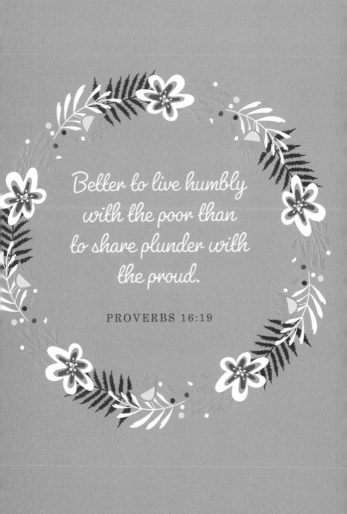

Better to live humbly
with the poor than
to share plunder with
the proud.

PROVERBS 16:19

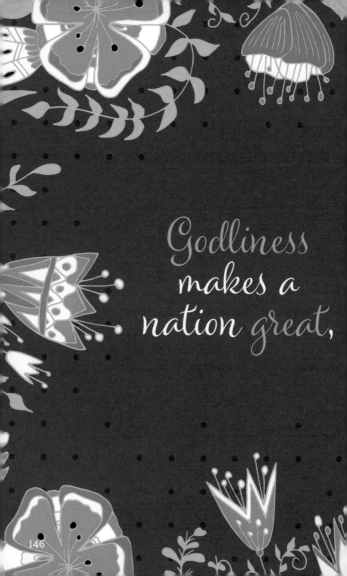

Godliness
makes a
nation great,

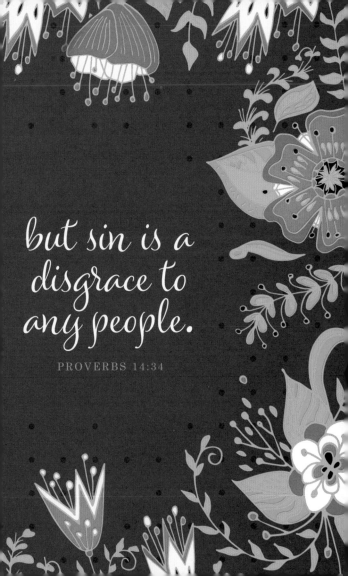

but sin is a
disgrace to
any people.

PROVERBS 14:34

One who has unreliable friends soon comes to ruin, but there is a friend who sticks closer than a brother.

PROVERBS 18:24, NIV

The wicked are
trapped by their own
words, but
*the godly escape
such trouble.*

PROVERBS 12:13

A person with good
sense is respected; a
treacherous person is
headed for destruction.

PROVERBS 13:15

The king's heart is in the hand of the LORD, as the rivers of water: he turneth it whithersoever he will.

PROVERBS 21:1, KJV

The words of the godly are a life-giving fountain; the words of the wicked conceal violent intentions.

PROVERBS 10:11

Folly is bound up in
the heart of a child,

but the rod of
discipline will drive
it far away.

PROVERBS 22:15, NIV

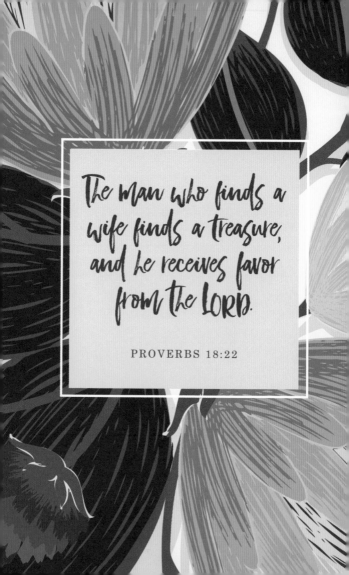

The man who finds a wife finds a treasure, and he receives favor from the LORD.

PROVERBS 18:22

Flipping a coin can end arguments; it settles disputes between powerful opponents. An offended friend is harder to win back than a fortified city. Arguments separate friends like a gate locked with bars.

PROVERBS 18:18-19

Don't rob the poor just because you can,
or exploit the needy in court. For the LORD
is their defender. He will ruin anyone who
ruins them.

PROVERBS 22:22-23

Wisdom is
enshrined in an
understanding
heart.

———

PROVERBS 14:33

Pride leads to disgrace, but with humility comes wisdom.

PROVERBS 11:2

People curse those who hoard their grain,
but they bless the one who sells in time of
need. If you search for good, you will find
favor; but if you search for evil, it will
find you!

PROVERBS 11:26-27

LIVING
EXPRESSIONS
COLLECTION

Living Expressions invites you to explore God's Word
and express your creativity in ways that are refreshing
to the spirit and restorative to the soul.

Visit Tyndale online at www.tyndale.com.

TYNDALE, Tyndale's quill logo, *Living Expressions*, and the Living
Expressions logo are registered trademarks of Tyndale House Publishers, Inc.

A Bouquet of Timeless Wisdom to Guide Your Path

For information about special discounts for bulk purchases, please contact
Tyndale House Publishers at csresponse@tyndale.com, or call 1-800-323-9400.

ISBN 978-1-4964-3604-7

Printed in China

24	23	22	21	20	19	18
7	6	5	4	3	2	1